SLOTHS

BY TYLER GRADY

Dylanna Press

Sloths are **mammals** that can be found in the tropical rainforests of Central America as well as northern parts of South America. Costa Rica is home to five million sloths and is one of the best places to see them in the wild.

Although some may think they are related to monkeys based on their long arms and tree-loving habits, sloths are xenarthrans and are most closely related to armadillos and anteaters. Their scientific name is *Folivora*, meaning leaf eater.

---

mammals – warm-blooded animals with hair or fur that give birth to live young

There are six different **species** of sloths that fall into two groups, two-toed or three-toed:

- Brown-throated sloth (three-toed)
- Hoffman's two-toed sloth
- Linnaeus's two-toed sloth
- Maned sloth (three-toed)
- Pale-throated sloth (three-toed)
- Pygmy three-toed sloth

The two-toed sloths measure around 21 to 29 inches (53 to 74 centimeters) and weigh 9 to 17 pounds (4 to 8 kilograms), they are roughly the size of a small dog. Three-toed sloths are a little smaller, with a length of about 18 to 25 inches (46 to 64 cm) and weight of 8-12 pounds (3.63 to 5.44 kg). Unlike two-toed sloths, they have short tails 2 to 3 inches (5-8 cm) in length.

Sloths sport long, coarse fur in shades of brown, long limbs accompanied by curved claws tailor-made for climbing trees and hanging upside down. They have round heads with small ears, a short snout, and brown eyes.

___

species – a group of animals that are alike and capable of reproducing together

Sloths are perfectly designed for their rainforest environment. While seemingly lazy and slow-moving, the sloth is in fact a masterpiece of evolution, tailored perfectly for life high in the trees of tropical rainforests.

One of its most notable physical adaptations is its impressively long and strong curved claws. These claws, which can measure up to 4 inches long in some species, enable the sloth to hook onto and hang from branches with ease. This adaptation not only allows sloths to feed on leaves that are out of reach for other herbivores, but it also lets them conserve energy by hanging relaxed and motionless, a strategy essential for an animal with such a low metabolic rate.

---

environment – surroundings, including all living and nonliving things, in a particular area that interact and affect each other

Another fascinating **adaptation** is their remarkable fur, which grows in the opposite direction compared to most mammals. Instead of growing from the back toward the belly, a sloth's fur grows from the belly toward the back. This unique growth pattern allows rain to easily run off their bodies, keeping them dry in their often damp rainforest home.

In addition, this fur houses **symbiotic** algae, providing the sloth with a greenish tint that acts as a camouflage against the leafy backdrop, making them almost invisible to potential predators.

---

adaptations – ways in which a species becomes fitted into its natural environment to increase its chance of survival

symbiotic – Close, mutually beneficial relationship between two different creatures

Sloths are **herbivores** and more specifically **folivores.** Their main diet consists of leaves, though some sloths also munch on fruits and buds. Because these rainforest trees have so many types of leaves, sloths will often choose just a few favorite kinds to nibble on. These leaves may not seem like much, but they provide the sloths with the nutrients they need to stay strong and healthy. However, there's a little secret: the leaves sloths love are often tough to digest and don't provide a lot of energy. But don't worry; sloths have a special trick up their sleeves!

To make the most out of their leafy meals, sloths have a very slow digestive process. Their stomachs are divided into multiple compartments, each with specific bacteria that help break down the tough leaves. This digestion takes a long time – sometimes, it can take up to a month for a sloth to fully digest a meal! Because this process requires so much energy and the leaves don't provide a quick boost, sloths are pretty sleepy creatures and need to rest a lot.

Even with their slow digestion, sloths don't eat very much. On average, they might eat just a small handful of leaves each day. But that's okay! Sloths have adapted to their environment and diet in such a way that they don't need a lot of food to keep them going.

---

herbivore – an animal that doesn't eat meat

folivore – an animal that exclusively or primary eats leaves

It's no secret that sloths love their nap time. Living high up in the rainforest canopies, sloths often curl up and sleep, comfortably suspended from tree branches with their powerful claws. The branches become their beds, providing them a secure place to rest without the need to come down to the forest floor often.

On average, sloths snooze away for about 15 to 20 hours a day! That's a lot, even compared to other animals known for their long sleeping habits.

Sloths are primarily **nocturnal**, meaning they are most active during the night. This nocturnal behavior allows them to go about their activities with fewer threats from potential predators that might be more active during the day. However, it's worth noting that sloths, given their slow pace and energy-conserving nature, do not have stark contrasts in activity levels between day and night. Even during their active periods at night, they move slowly and do not travel great distances. During the day, while they might be resting more, it's still possible to see a sloth awake and moving about, especially if it's overcast or cooler. But in general, the majority of their more active behaviors, like feeding, will occur under the cover of night.
_____

nocturnal – active at night, asleep during the day

Sloths

are solitary animals, and while they have a home range, they don't have territories in the aggressive, strictly defended sense that some other animals do. Their home ranges can vary depending on the abundance of food, the type of forest, and the species of sloth.

Sloths aren't **nomadic**, but they aren't really **territorial** either. They do move around within their home ranges, but they don't migrate long distances. Their slow pace and specialized diet mean that they tend to stay in areas where they know they can find their preferred types of leaves. Additionally, because sloths have such a slow metabolism and digestive process, they don't need to constantly search for food like some other animals.

Female sloths tend to be more sedentary than males, sticking to a specific set of trees that they know well and that provide them with adequate food. Males might roam a bit more, especially in search of potential mates, but even this movement is relatively limited given their energy-conserving lifestyle.

So, while sloths will move from tree to tree in search of food and might venture out for mating opportunities, they generally stay within familiar areas and do not roam vast distances or lead a nomadic lifestyle.

---

nomadic – an animal that moves from place to place

territorial – an animal that defends an area against others of its species

Sloths are solitary by nature, but when it's time to find a mate, females initiate the process by emitting a high-pitched scream. This call lets nearby males know that she's ready to mate. Sloths are not **monogamous** and both males and females will have multiple mates.

Sloths mate year round and the **gestation period** varies depending on the species. For the three-toed sloth, it's around six months, while the two-toed sloth can have a longer period of up to 12 months.

Usually, a female will give birth to just one baby at a time. These little ones are born fairly well-developed, with their eyes open and claws ready to cling. In fact, shortly after birth, baby sloths cling to their mother's belly, providing them with a mobile safety net as she navigates through the trees.

---

monogamous – to have only one mate
gestation period – length of pregnancy

Parenting among sloths is primarily the mother's duty. The father doesn't play a role in raising the young. As for the mother, she is dedicated, nursing her baby with milk and keeping it close for warmth and protection.

The young sloth will remain with its mother for six months up to a year, learning the essential skills of survival. This includes knowing which leaves are best to eat and how to maneuver through the dense canopy.

Once they're old enough, these young sloths will venture out to find their own home range, continuing the slow-paced cycle of life in the treetops.

Sloths play a crucial role in the intricate web of their rainforest ecosystem. The slow movement of sloths through the treetops helps in the dispersion of seeds and nutrients. As they feed on various leaves, fruits, and buds, they aid in the spread of plant seeds throughout the forest. Their waste, once it falls to the ground, enriches the soil, promoting plant growth, aiding in forest regeneration, and promoting plant **diversity**.

Sloths are often likened to a "mobile ecosystem." Their fur is home to a variety of insects and microorganisms, including moths, beetles, and fungi. The so-called "sloth moths" even lay their eggs in sloth dung, and the larvae feed on it. When the moths mature, they fly up into the canopy, seeking out other sloths.

---

diversity – variation in living things in an ecosystem

While sloths are primarily known for their slow-paced, solitary lifestyle, they aren't entirely without social interactions or methods of communication. Though they don't form large social groups like some other mammals, their interactions are subtle yet essential for their survival and reproduction.

- **Mating Calls:** When a female sloth is ready to mate, she emits a distinct, high-pitched scream or call to attract males in the area. This vocalization is a clear invitation for potential mates to approach, and can sometimes even lead to rival males competing for her attention.
- **Mother-Offspring Bond:** After giving birth, the young sloth will emit soft calls or whistles, especially if it feels threatened or is separated from its mother. This vocal communication ensures the baby remains close and protected, especially during its vulnerable early months.
- **Defensive Hisses:** If threatened or cornered, a sloth might hiss or emit a sharp vocalization to ward off potential predators or threats.
- **Physical Interactions:** Males may swipe at each other with their long claws during confrontations over territory or mating rights. These physical confrontations, while slow-paced, are a clear form of communication, establishing dominance or territory.
- **Chemical Communication:** It's believed that sloths, like many other animals, use scent marking to communicate. By leaving behind their scent, they can convey information about their presence, territory, or reproductive status to other sloths.
- **Facial Expressions:** While not as pronounced as in some animals, sloths do use facial expressions to communicate, especially when feeling threatened. Wide eyes and a bared-tooth snarl can be a warning sign that a sloth feels cornered or endangered.

Despite their reputation as solitary creatures, these forms of communication show that sloths do engage in social interactions, even if they're more subdued compared to other animals. Whether it's finding a mate, protecting their young, or simply conveying their mood, sloths have their own unique ways of "talking" to the world around them.

With a lifespan of around 20 to 30 years in the wild, sloths enjoy relatively lengthy lives for a mammal their size.

Among the six sloth species, two are considered **endangered species**. The Pygmy Three-Toed Sloth is critically endangered, while the Maned Three-Toed Sloth is classified as vulnerable.

Sloths, with their slow pace and treetop habitats, face several predators and other threats in their rainforest environment.

One of the most formidable **predators** of sloths, particularly in the Amazon rainforest, is the harpy eagle. This powerful bird of prey has keen eyesight, enabling it to spot a sloth from high up in the sky and swiftly swoop down to snatch it from the tree canopy. On the rare occasions when sloths descend to the forest floor they are at risk of being caught by land predators such as jaguars and ocelots.

---

endangered species – in danger of disappearing forever

predators – animal that hunts other animals for food

Humans are one of the biggest threats to sloths. The most severe threat is due to habitat loss caused by **deforestation**. Human activity, such as logging and clear-cutting for agriculture, is rapidly destroying the rainforests that sloths call home.

In regions where their habitat intersects with human settlements, sloths sometimes mistake power lines for trees or vines. Electrocution from these power lines is a modern hazard for these creatures.

Road accidents are another human-related danger. As deforestation and development encroach on sloth territories, sloths sometimes find themselves needing to cross roads. Their slow movement makes them particularly vulnerable to being hit by vehicles.

Additionally, sloths are sometimes captured for the illegal pet trade or killed for their claws and fur.

Climate change is another threat to sloths. Rising temperatures and changing ecosystems have had a negative effect on rainforests and pose a significant challenge for sloths.

---

deforestation – the purposeful clearing of forested land

climate change – long-term changes in expected weather patterns

Sloths are some of the most intriguing inhabitants of the rainforest. From their deliberate, slow-motion movements to their unique role as mobile ecosystems, these creatures captivate the imagination. Their seemingly laid-back demeanor belies remarkable adaptations that have evolved over millions of years, enabling them to survive and thrive in one of the planet's most diverse and complex environments.

However, sloths face an uncertain future. As the modern world encroaches upon their habitats, they must navigate challenges that their evolutionary history did not prepare them for, from deforestation to roadways. The good news is that as awareness grows about these gentle tree-dwellers, so does global interest in protecting them.

In the balance between nature's design and human impact, sloths stand as a poignant reminder of the delicate web of life. Their continued existence hinges on the choices we make as stewards of the planet. But with collaborative conservation efforts and a dedication to sustainable coexistence, there is hope that future generations will still be able to gaze up into the canopy and witness the mesmerizing slow dance of the sloth.

Word Search

```
J R Z C P E C O S Y S T E M F
Q V B I V N O I T U L O V E N
N O I T A C I N U M M O C F Y
T A I Y I T E R R I T O R Y N
N R C I S E P S E V A E L O F
E V G S Y J X R Q D K H I S O
M I R L M C C R E E G T O S L
N A H A B P X S A D A Q K F I
O D S M I R Q G O T A A T Y V
R A E M O N L Y S L L T T E O
I P I A S A F E P A I I O N R
V T C M I S R O N S S T U R A
N A E N S O L R R R K A A C S
E T P T F O U E E E D M Z R N
M I S E B T Z V E Z S E M D Y
S O D K C B I E G P X T B F W
U N S O S D N O I T S E G I D
C S N H E R B I V O R E S T C
```

ADAPTATIONS   ENVIRONMENT   PREDATORS
ALGAE   EVOLUTION   RAINFOREST
COMMUNICATION   FOLIVORA   SLEEP
DEFORESTATION   HERBIVORES   SOLITARY
DIGESTION   LEAVES   SPECIES
DIVERSITY   MAMMALS   SYMBIOSIS
ECOSYSTEM   NOCTURNAL   TERRITORY

INDEX

activity levels, 15
adaptations, 8, 11, 31
algae, 11
claws, 7, 8
climate change, 28
communication, 24
Costa Rica, 4
defenses, 24
deforestation, 28, 31
diet, 8, 12
digestion, 12
diversity, 23
eating habits, 8, 12
ecosystem, 23, 28, 31
endangered species, 27
environment, 8
facial expressions, 24
Folivora, 4
folivores, 12
fur, 7, 11, 23
future challenges, 31
gestation period, 19
habitat, 4
harpy eagle, 27
herbivores, 12
humans, 28, 31
jaguars, 27
lifespan, 27
mammals, 4
mating, 16, 19, 24

microorganisms, 23
moths, 23
nocturnal, 15
nomadic, 16
ocelots, 27
offspring, 19, 20, 24
parenting, 19, 20, 24
pet trade, 28
physical adaptations, 8, 11, 31
physical characteristics, 7
power lines, 28
predators, 11, 27
rainforests, 4, 23
reproduction, 19
road accidents, 28
scent marking, 24
size, 7
sleep, 15
social interactions, 16, 19, 24
solitary, 19
species, 7
symbiotic relationships, 11
territory, 16, 24
threats, 27, 28
three-toed sloths, 7
two-toed sloths, 7
vocalizations, 24
xenarthrans, 4

Published by Dylanna Press an imprint of Dylanna Publishing, Inc.
Copyright © 2023 by Dylanna Press
Author: Tyler Grady
All rights reserved. No part of this publication may be reproduced, stored in a retrieval system, or transmitted by any means, including electronic, mechanical, photocopying, or otherwise, without prior written permission of the publisher.

Although the publisher has taken all reasonable care in the preparation of this book, we make no warranty about the accuracy or completeness of its content and, to the maximum extent permitted, disclaim all liability arising from its use.

Printed in the U.S.A.

Printed in Great Britain
by Amazon